Air

ENVIRONMENT
COLLECTION FOR KIDS

Israel Felzenszwalb · David Palatnik

Air

Illustrations by
David Palatnik

Hi,

nice to meet you! I'm AIR.

You can't see me?

That's good news! It means I'm clean!

4

YOUR LIFE DEPENDS ON ME.

Do you know why?

You need to

BREATHE

ME

IN ORDER

TO LIVE!

I'm made of a mixture of several different kinds of gases with funny names: nitrogen, oxygen, carbon dioxide and others.

I cover the whole planet Earth with a VERY THIN LAYER called the ATMOSPHERE. That's why...

Atmosphere

Earth

...the higher you go the harder it is to breathe. Smart mountain climbers already know that.

It is also because of me that the sky is BLUE!
I like it, do you?

When you INHALE me, I enter your body through your nose or mouth and go straight to your lungs. And when you EXHALE me, some of me goes back into the ATMOSPHERE. This INHALE and EXHALE movement is called BREATHING.

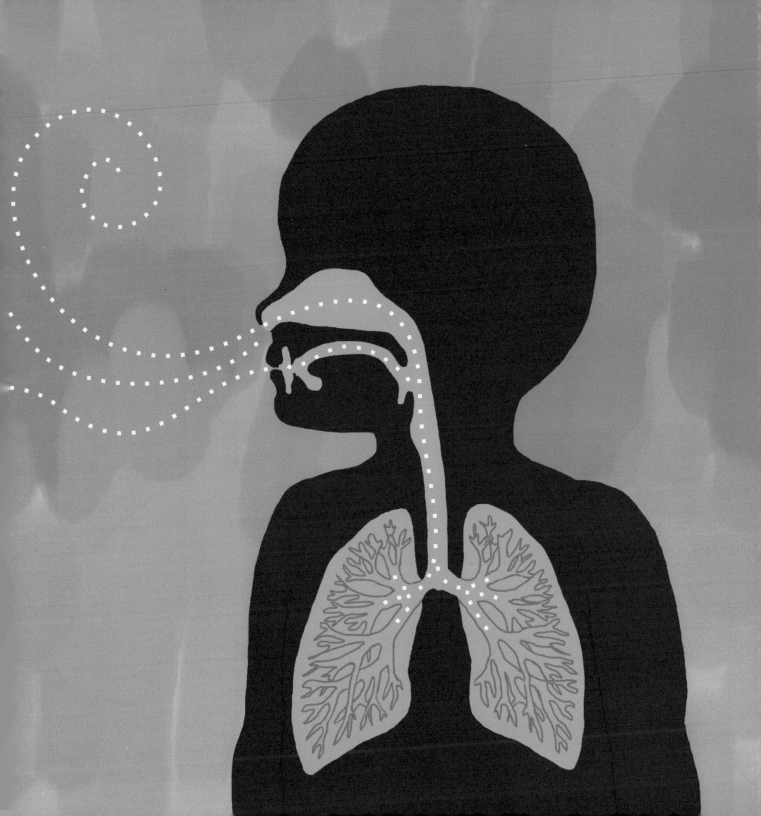

The OXYGEN that I carry goes into your blood and, together with the FOOD you eat, produces the ENERGY you need to live.

You can go a long time without eating, but try to stay one minute without breathing! OW, it's hard!

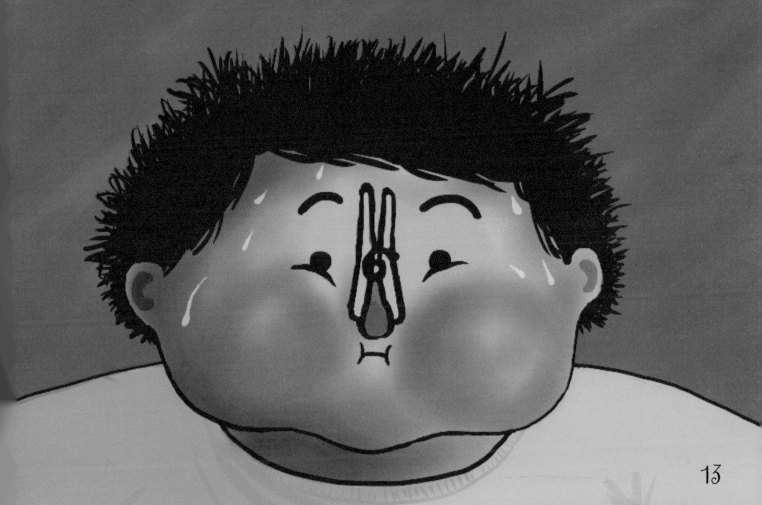

DID YOU KNOW THAT:

- When I get trapped in your stomach it makes you burp?

- Wind is generated when a layer of hot air is replaced by a layer of cold air?

- Fire needs oxygen in order to burn?

Look at all the things
I am used for:

Travelling by balloon

Livening up a party

Helping put out a fire

Filling the car tire

Diving

Walking in space

Painting

But most important of all,
I ALWAYS NEED TO BE VERY CLEAN!

Unfortunately, cars, trucks, planes, factories, refineries, the burning of waste, and even people smoking ARE POLLUTING ME A LOT!

This is bad not just for you, but also for ANIMALS and PLANTS: they need CLEAN AIR to breathe too!

Some steps are already being taken to improve the situation. For instance: electric cars, filters for factories, garbage recycling, giving up smoking.

KEEP YOUR CITY CLEAN

Perhaps you can think of ways
to make me cleaner, too.
The Earth and everyone on it
would be so grateful!

ABOUT THE COLLECTION

This Collection is the result of an encounter between two brazilian friends who had not seen each other for more than forty years. One is a biologist, the other an art director and illustrator. Both had the same idea: to combine an amusing text with captivating pictures to make children understand the multidisciplinary questions that arise with regard to the study and perception of the environment. They are driven by the conviction that if we are to protect our planet we have to start working from childhood onwards to change the paradigms.

Israel Felzenszwalb & David Palatnik

See also the other books from this collection:

Plants

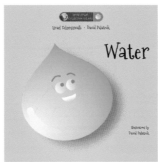

Water

Earth

Printed in Great Britain
by Amazon

44025322R00018